THE SIOUX INDIANS

THE SIOUX
INDIANS

HUNTERS AND WARRIORS
OF THE PLAINS

11680

By SONIA BLEEKER
Illustrated by KISA SASAKI

WILLIAM MORROW & COMPANY
New York, 1962

13   14   15

Grateful recognition is given to Dr. Gordon MacGregor of Falls Church, Virginia, for reading and criticizing the manuscript.

CONTENTS

THE SIOUX INDIANS

I

THE SIOUX

THE SIOUX INDIANS, the greatest warriors of the plains, today call North and South Dakota their homelands. They were latecomers into this far western territory. Tribes of the Sioux Indians first began to move into the Great Plains from about 1750 to 1775—just before the American Revolution. It seemed a time of general unrest among the Indian people, as well as among non-Indians. Hard pressed by the Chippewa Indians, the Sioux were forced to move to the Great Plains. They took a liking to the new land and to the free, adventurous life of buffalo hunters and warriors. Later they became outstanding horsemen.

So far as we have learned from the memory of old men among the Sioux and from old men of other Indian people, the Sioux originally lived on or near the Mississippi River in southern Minnesota, Wisconsin, and northern Iowa. These lands abounded in lakes and rivers, so the ancestors of the Sioux were woodland hunters, fishermen, and canoemen. Their women gathered the wild rice that grew in abundance in the shallow lakes, made maple syrup in the spring, and tended their small fields of corn, beans, squash, and sunflowers. The younger men helped clear the fields, and the older men tended small patches of tobacco to be used in ceremonies. Most of the year the men were free to trap beaver and to war with their neighbors.

Their beautiful, bountiful lands, with clear lakes, rivers, and streams, had sufficient game and fish for everyone, but warring seemed also to be a part of the Indians' way of life. One group would push another out of its villages and occupy them. After a time the weaker group found allies and returned to push out the conquerers. In turn, the conquered bided their time, healed their wounds, acquired their own allies, and went back to try and regain the lost ground.

The stories told by the old men among the Sioux and by their enemies, the Chippewa, are full of these battles. They all began with the surprise attack at dawn. Women and children fled for cover into the woods or jumped into swift canoes to escape. Warriors remained behind to defend their wigwams or tipis. The enemy burned the village. There were scalp dances among the victors, and mourning and gashing of their bodies in sorrow among the defeated. The homeless found shelter with relatives in other villages or among other tribes, and planned revenge.

In between the battles, there were long periods of peace. Chiefs from both sides would gather in council, talk over the wrongs, and smoke the peace pipe. Each side promised to maintain the peace and not be the first one to break it. Time would go by, and the Sioux villages and the Chippewa villages would enjoy the relaxation of peace. Men no longer kept watch for enemy attacks. The Sioux scouts slept peacefully inside their tipis.

The former enemies visited and feasted together. Sioux even married Chippewa girls, and Chippewa men married Sioux girls.

Then some incident would take place, and the fighting would flare up again. The villages were turned into armed camps, with the men always on the alert for an attack and the women and children ready to flee. Yet the young men on both sides seemed to enjoy this life of danger, or they would not have carried it on for so many centuries.

When, in the seventeenth century, the Chippewa acquired guns and gunpowder from the white men, they became stronger than their Sioux enemies, and within a century were able to oust them from their homelands. It must have been very hard for the Sioux to leave their rich lands and the graves of their fathers. But many of them were horsemen by this time. And many had had the experience of hunting buffalo—especially the young warriors, who had already made sorties onto the plains and knew something of their vastness. So this tragic departure from their homes turned out rather well for the Sioux

Of course, we do not know all the details of these early migrations, nor how long they took. Every people, no matter how well-prepared, suffers when forced to leave its homeland. There are always old people—old fathers and mothers—to whom travel is a hardship. There are always mothers with infants, who must travel slowly, with frequent and long stopovers. On these long marches, groups have to camp for long periods, so the men may hunt. The women dry the freshly killed meat, tan skins, and sew clothing and moccasins to replace those that are worn out. Although the Sioux began to move into the Great Plains after 1750, they moved slowly, and did not reach the Black Hills in western South Dakota until around 1780. At first they wandered along the river valleys, where there were trees and shrubs for shelter and firewood. They planted crops and stayed in the same place until they harvested them. Then gradually they came to the high plains and gave up farming.

It must have been a shock to the majority of these woodland people when they faced the openness of the plains and prairies. Woodland people are used to landmarks—clusters of permanent houses and villages, clusters of trees and woods, meadows, streams, and lakes. The vastness of the Great Plains must have overwhelmed these newcomers at first. On the plains—in all four directions—was rolling land, covered with grass and shrubs and surrounded by the horizon. Without landmarks, men could easily get lost.

From the tragic accounts left us by the Spanish invaders under Coronado, we know how difficult it was to travel on the Great Plains. Yet Coronado possessed a compass. Scribes followed him, mapping the region and keeping records of the distances covered. He moved cautiously, yet tragedy followed him daily. Some of Coronado's scouts got lost and never returned. They perished of hunger and thirst after days of wandering. Even in the nineteenth century travelers reported that they almost lost their minds walking over the Great Plains. The scenery was exactly the same day after day, till men began to doubt whether they were moving forward at all.

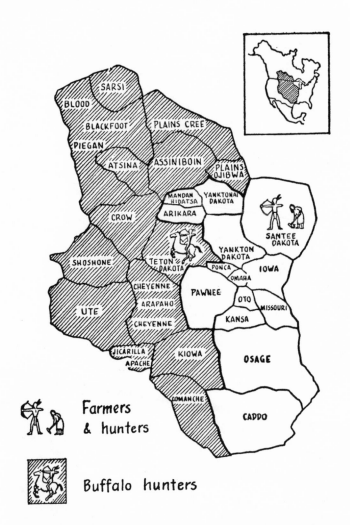

SARSI
BLOOD
BLACKFOOT
PIEGAN
ATSINA
PLAINS CREE
ASSINIBOIN
PLAINS OJIBWA
MANDAN HIDATSA
YANKTONAI DAKOTA
ARIKARA
CROW
SANTEE DAKOTA
YANKTON DAKOTA
SHOSHONE
TETON DAKOTA
PONCA
IOWA
OMAHA
CHEYENNE
PAWNEE
OTO
MISSOURI
ARAPAHO
UTE
KANSA
CHEYENNE
JICARILLA APACHE
KIOWA
OSAGE
COMANCHE
CADDO

Farmers & hunters

Buffalo hunters

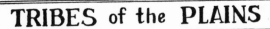

TRIBES of the PLAINS

The Sioux eventually mastered this difficulty, but not perhaps without loss of life. Traveling over a new region, a hunter or group of hunters on horseback started out with the sunrise. Moving westward, away from the sun, they shot an arrow ahead of them, to make sure they were going in a straight line. Shooting arrow after arrow while watching the sun, they made sure of their direction. Returning to camp at sunset, they again shot their arrows, eastward this time, to make sure they were returning in the same direction. In time, they learned the new landmarks. The wide buffalo trails were a help, and the men often piled stone and brush and buffalo skulls as markers at crossroads.

Between the Mississippi and the Rockies and from northern Texas to Canada the Great Plains are flat. The land rises from east to west, from 1000 to 5000 feet above sea level. The highest region is the Black Hills of South Dakota. The temperature varies in summer from a hot 100 degrees in Texas to a cool 75 degrees in North Dakota. The hot sun is equally unbearable to man and buffalo. There is little rainfall during the summer. The vegetation is low—bushes, sage, and bunch grass. There are always open, barren spots all over the dry areas. In stretches, where the spring rains do not run off the surface immediately, there are patches of fresh green grass. Otherwise, the vegetation is a pale green-gray.

When the tall grass of the plains moved with the winds, it was probably very much like the ocean, quaking, moving restlessly. On windless, sunny days, when the grass was at rest, the vast plain probably resembled the glassy evenness of an ocean under quiet skies. And over this vastness roamed tremendous herds of buffalo—counted in the millions. There were also elk, deer, antelope, wolves, and coyotes. There were birds of all kinds, including eagles and vultures, and in the spring the plains were breeding grounds for ducks, coots, plovers, sandpipers, and others.

The Sioux soon learned the ways of the plains and the way of life that made the most of what the plains offered—buffalo. They became nomads, and followed the buffalo migrations. They soon forgot their farming, their sod houses, their birchbark canoes. Their religious beliefs now included the spirits that guarded the buffalo and guided the hunters season after season. The Sioux raided for horses and traded for horses. They became Plains Indians in every way.

The name Sioux is a French corruption of the original Algonkia name for these tribes. The original name was Nadouessioux, which means enemy. In the language of their enemies, the Chippewa, Nadouessioux means rattlesnake. The French traders evidently found it hard to pronounce the full word and shortened it to Sioux (soo).

The Nadouessioux were made up of many groups or tribes, speaking related dialects. The simplest way to show these tribal divisions is to divide them into geographic blocks—the Santee or Eastern Sioux, who reached into Minnesota; the middle group, made up of the Yankton and Yanktonai; and the third group, which was called the Western or Teton Dakota.

After they entered the plains, the Sioux tribes formed an alliance among themselves. They became known as the Dakota, or Allies, and their language was Siouan.

The Sioux became famous for their horsemanship and elaborate ceremonial dress. They were thin and tall (many were six-footers), and had large noses and large hands and feet. The men's buckskin shirts and leggings were fringed, and decorated with scalp locks and porcupine quills. They wore breastplates of shell, necklaces of bear claws, earrings, and arm bands. Their moccasins, with tough soles of buffalo hide, were also elaborately worked with porcupine quills, and dyed in bright colors of red, yellow, and blue. The men carried themselves with great dignity. The feathers they wore in their long hair added to their impressive height.

On festive and important occasions, when they appeared in councils, chiefs wore buffalo robes and long headdresses of eagle feathers. The crown of the feather headdress was often finished with mink. The legs and tail of the mink hung down on either side of the warrior's face.

During their war dances the Sioux liked to boast about their brave deeds. They were not shy like some of the Pueblo Indians, for example. Each Sioux man, no matter how old or how young, wanted everyone in the audience to know him for what he had achieved.

The Sioux women were also tall. They dressed in ankle-length buckskin dresses, with fringes at the hem, sides, and sleeves. In addition, a woman decorated her dress with porcupine quills, and later with beads and buttons acquired by trading. Each dress was made of two beautifully tanned deerskins. Their moccasins were also very elaborate.

Little boys and girls dressed like their parents, although at first little boys wore only long shirts. Up to the age of seven and eight they stayed close to their mother and the tipi. The little girls played with tiny tipis and dolls, the boys with small spears, bows and blunt arrows, shields, and sticks. Theirs was a carefree life, full of fun and games.

The father took little notice of the boys, although he enjoyed playing with them when he was at home. During dances, games, and festivals, the father sat with the other men, and the children watched the ceremonies with their mother from the sidelines.

When a boy reached eight, he joined the circle of growing boys, who gathered to listen to an old man. This was their schooling. The old man taught the small boys, repeating over and over again what the Sioux thought was most important in life—that it was better to die young, while you were still in full health and power, than to live a long life and be poor, sick, and dependent on others. Freedom and independence made life worth living. After a life of bravery and adventure on earth, a man entered the eternal life among the spirits. There he remained the same age as when he died, and continued the good life of hunting and warring he had had on earth. A boy never forgot these lessons. He was a Sioux, destined to become a fearless hunter and warrior.

Just as the children sat in a circle listening to

the old man, their father sat in a circle in the councils that discussed the plans and problems of each camp, listening and sometimes—if he had earned the honor—being permitted to get up and speak. The Sioux were very democratic. All men had a voice in deciding about hunting and when to go on the warpath. But if a person was young, inexperienced, and had not earned any fame, either as a hunter or as a warrior and raider, he remained silent.

In times of peace a Sioux camp was full of noise, gaiety, and laughter. There were children playing games in front of every tipi. Children practiced horseback riding at every opportunity. Little girls rode as well as the little boys. Outside the circle of tipis older boys were busy, racing their horses, wrestling, and practicing with their bows and arrows.

As a boy grew older and more skilled with the spear and bow, his father or grandfather made him arrows that were pointed. He could now practice with moving targets instead of the stationary targets of his childhood days. This helped

to train him for shooting at game on the move. Soon after, the young man began to make his own weapons, which were man-sized now, and he was ready to join a war party.

Older girls stayed close to their tipis, busy with housework. Girls and women were responsible for gathering dried buffalo chips for the fires. They carried water from the spring or river. They skinned and tanned the hides of all the buffalo the

men of the household killed. They sewed, embroidered, and mended clothing and moccasins for
themselves and their menfolk. They dried all the
buffalo meat and cooked the meals. Mats from
the tipi floor and walls were dusted and left outside to dry in the sun. People knew when a woman
turned a tipi inside out that her husband was
planning a feast—perhaps to celebrate a boy's return from a successful buffalo hunt by giving him

a new name, or perhaps to distribute gifts for a daughter, who was ready for marriage.

Amidst this activity, there was the quiet beating of drums. Inside the tipis men practiced their songs for a dance, or just played the drum and sang for their own amusement.

The busiest and hardest working people in each camp were the old women. It was their lot to tan the many buffalo skins for robes. Although a buffalo robe lasted a lifetime, it was also a good article of trade among the Plains Indians, so there was always need for more of them. Younger women did not like to labor over the tanning. The fatty mixture of brains and urine used in tanning was very hard on a woman's hands, and the younger women wanted their hands kept pretty. Older women were not as vain about their appearance and the softness of their hands.

While these activities were taking place in different tipis, one tipi might be closed. A woman outside it motioned to the children to keep away. Such a tipi, usually located in the center of the camp, was the soldiers' lodge.

In each large Sioux camp there was a small group of men, called soldiers or policemen. They were mature men who had proved themselves good hunters and warriors—men of courage and responsibility. Their special tipi was always located in the center of the camp next to the chief's tipi. Here men met to discuss the business of the camp and to plan for its welfare. Visitors to the camp stayed in this tipi. Young hunters gladly donated the tongues of the deer or buffalo they shot for a feast at the soldiers' lodge. But until they proved themselves, young men could not enter this lodge. Nor were women permitted to enter. They cooked the men's food outside the tipi, and also left firewood, or buffalo chips, and water for them there.

The business inside the lodge was not always of a serious nature, however. When there were no problems to tackle, the men amused themselves by telling stories, playing games, and working on their weapons, their shields, their pipes, and ornaments. At such times, the soldiers' lodge was full of laughter and noise just like the rest of the camp.

The camp chief was also jolly and was always ready to play gambling games with the policemen and warriors. But outside the tipi the chief appeared solemn and cut a figure of great dignity, as befits a man who is called Father and who calls everyone in camp his child.

In the very large camps there were other lodges, which belonged to various secret societies to which men belonged. Here the members met to discuss their business, to initiate new members, and to plan for their part in forthcoming ceremonies.

As early as 1750 the Sioux were already one of the largest groups among the Plains Indians. Their population was then about 25,000, a mighty nation, which controlled great hunting territories. The buffalo was abundant.

2

SEARCH FOR POWER

To INSURE good health and success in buffalo hunting and in war, it was most important that each man try to get special power from his guardian spirit through a dream or a vision. This was one of the many religious beliefs of the Sioux. Some of these beliefs are hard for us to understand as it is hard for the average Indian to understand ours.

Indians in the early days believed that everything—every object—had a life of its own. They believed that rocks, trees, birds, and animals possessed souls or spirits. These spirits could remain invisible, or change at will to become birds, animals, or men. All spirits had this power to change shape at will.

In the Siouan beliefs all animals were sent to the plains by the Great Spirit, Wakan Tanka, as food for the Sioux. Birds, the Winged Beings, were held in great esteem. The Sioux turned to the Winged Beings in their prayers. They were closest to the Great Spirit, since they were able to fly.

An important legend of the Sioux is the one of the White Buffalo Cow Maiden, who first gave the Sioux the calumet, or peace pipe, and taught them about it. Calumet is a French word, which means *peace*.

The White Buffalo Cow Maiden first appeared to two Sioux hunters as a beautiful girl, and asked the two hunters to lead her to their camp. The maiden taught their chief and all the people about the sacredness of the calumet and told them that the men who smoked it together must promise to live in peace. She then placed the calumet in the chief's hands and left the lodge. The people watched her go. A short distance from the tipi the maiden stopped. She lay down on the ground and turned into a buffalo calf. A while later, as the astonished people watched, she lay down again, rolled over, and arose as a white buffalo. Some Sioux had seen white buffalo—albinos—before. Many kinds of animals gave birth to albino offspring, but because they were different from their parents, the Indians always regarded albinos with some fear and respect. A white buffalo was an unusual sight. As the people continued watching, the white buffalo lay down once more, rolled over, and became a dark buffalo.

From these earliest days, when a young man wanted to get extra power in a vision, he carried with him the sacred pipe, with its long stem made of wood that had been hollowed out in the center. The pipe itself was such an important religious symbol that the Plains Indians who smoked it to seal a promise of peace among themselves were called the Indians of the Calumet.

The pipe bowl was made of a red stone, which has been named catlinite in honor of a white man, George Catlin. For some eight years (from 1832 to 1839) George Catlin traveled among the Indian tribes of North America, and painted portraits of them, of their camps, their country, and their activities. He saw the sacred red stone calumets the Indians smoked in ceremonies, and wanted to find out where the stone was quarried. Catlin finally succeeded in visiting the quarry in southwestern Minnesota.

For many centuries catlinite had been quarried there by Plains Indians, who came and camped for several days at a time and chipped away with stone axes at the comparatively thin layer of red stone, which was only three or four inches thick. The peculiarity of this stone is that it is rather soft when newly quarried, and can be chipped easily, but after a while it hardens. So it was not too difficult to make it into pipe bowls. The beauty of the red stone, with white veins running through it, appealed to the Indians.

At the time Catlin saw it, the quarry was under the control of the Sioux Indians. They were naturally suspicious, because the quarry, too, was considered sacred, and they did not want white men to trespass the sacred grounds. The stone, they believed, had turned red from the blood of the buffalo, which Wakan Tanka hunted and killed for his food. The many groups of Indians, who camped near the quarry, always maintained peace, even though they were bitter enemies at home. Many carved their sacred symbols on nearby rocks in memory of their stay at the quarry.

This place, now called Pipestone Quarry, is in Pipestone County, Minnesota, and it is still reserved for Indians, who come here to get the stone for their pipes. The town that has grown up nearby is also called Pipestone.

A Sioux youth, in search of sacred power, usually asked for an old and wise man's help. Everyone knew that it was important to proceed with care in contacting the spirits. A mishandling might bring misfortune, not only upon the young man and his family, but upon the entire camp. The young man brought his calumet with him when he came to speak to the old man.

First of all, the old man and a few younger

helpers built a small sweat lodge. Men had to purify themselves in the sweat lodge, so they might speak of sacred things. It had to be built very carefully, step by step, as the ritual prescribed. Even cutting the dozen or so slender willows for the frame was done with care. The young man sprinkled tobacco and spoke to the saplings. "There are many kinds of trees here, but I have chosen you to help me. Many more will grow in your place." The rocks and the little bundle of twigs used for the fire in the sweat lodge were also spoken to with prayers.

The low sweat lodge was a simple structure. The saplings were bent into shape and tied at the top. A buffalo robe was placed over the framework. Inside the sweat lodge the old man drew lines, joining the four directions. The lines looked like a cross, and its center was sacred. It represented the center of the universe. The calumet, with its stem pointing up, was placed in the center of the sweat lodge. It meant that earth and sky were now joined. The inside of the sweat lodge represented a large cave. From this cave each

spring came the buffalo herds, so that the Sioux might hunt and live.

One of the men lit the small fire inside the sweat lodge. One by one, they rubbed themselves with little bundles of sage, which they had held over the fire as the old man chanted prayers. This rubbing purified the men. They also placed by the fire a bag of earth, so the earth on which they walked would be purified. If they were thirsty, the men were permitted to drink all they wanted, but the young man in search of the vision had to be careful not to spill the water he was drinking.

That would be wasting it, and wasting precious water always angered the Thunder Beings. If so angered, these Thunder Beings might later try to test the young man's stamina, to frighten him. A person in search of a vision must not be afraid of anything.

After the purification ceremony, the young man and his two friends and helpers left their camp and rode away to a hilltop, where he planned to stay for two or three days and nights, awaiting a vision. The two helpers rode up to the top first to prepare a good place for the young man. They saw to it that he had a level platform, on which to walk as he prayed, and a tree to lean on when he felt weak and could no longer stand up, or when he wanted to crouch down for a short nap. The helpers also left a buffalo robe for him to use as a cover in case of cold or rain.

When all was ready for him, the vision seeker climbed slowly up to his station, and his helpers left him. He stripped off his breechcloth, so he would appear poor before the spirits and deserve their pity. Carrying his pipe before him, the young man cried and prayed, "O Great Spirit, have pity on me that my people may live." He walked around the platform hour after hour, crying and praying. At the same time he was alert for any signs from the spirits. A bird that had just alighted on a nearby tree stump might be carrying a message for him, or even an ant might be a messenger. Birds, of course, were watched more closely, because they were nearest to the spirits. As the sun set, the tired young man might lie down for a while to rest, but after a short nap, he had to get up and continue walking around and praying. On the second and third day, as he got hungrier and weaker, he might remain in a crouching position near the tree.

The young man tried to keep track of all that took place day after day, because he would have to recount to the holy man all that he saw and felt during the days of vigil. Every happening had two meanings to the young man—that which he saw in an ordinary way and the second and hidden meaning, which the wise old man would interpret for him.

By this time, the young man was faint from hunger. He heard strange sounds in the quiet of his high retreat. The trees seemed to have a special way of whispering, and he listened closely, even though he did not understand the hidden language of the trees. At night birds called and made other noises, which he tried to memorize, so he might repeat them and get their hidden meanings. He was so busy watching and memorizing these happenings that he had no time to be afraid. The sky was clouding, and the Thunder Beings would be about during the night.

And so the four days and wakeful nights passed, and the helpers at last came to fetch him back to camp. The young man was hungry, thirsty, and weak. But nonetheless, he noticed with pride that the helpers thought he had held up well. They helped him mount his horse, which had been grazing quietly below, where the helpers had hobbled it. They all returned to the sweat lodge. The fire was burning, and the old man greeted the vision seeker and warned him, before

he began to speak, that the animals of the hillside had witnessed all that happened to him.
He must, therefore, be sure to tell exactly all that
took place. He must tell the dreams he had had
while he napped, and he must speak the truth, because the sacred pipe was present.

The young man unburdened himself of all the
impressions he had accumulated and memorized
during the four lonely days and nights. The old
man listened carefully. Afterward, he interpreted
the meanings of everything the young man had
seen and felt. He had gained power, the old man
assured him. The eagle that he had seen soaring
over his head was a good omen. Now the young
man was ready to rest and eat. He would seek
another vision to gain still more sacred power at
another time—perhaps a winter or two later.

Oftentimes a Sioux youth might have a vision
without much preparation. This happened to the
famous Sioux chief, Sitting Bull, when he was
only about fourteen winters old. He was, of course,
a remarkable boy. At fourteen he had killed a buf-

falo and fought in a war party against Crow enemies, which earned him the honorary name of
Sitting Bull.

Sitting Bull told the story of his vision in a special record he kept in pictographs on a buffalo
robe. Such records were kept by some men for
counting years. Sitting Bull was hunting not far
from camp for small game. He was alone and on
foot. The sun was hot overhead, and he got tired
of walking. He found a shady tree and lay down
to rest. As he dozed off, Sitting Bull thought he
heard a rustling among the branches. But before
he could open his eyes, a bird knocked several
times against the trunk of the tree. The knock said,
"Be still, be still."

Sitting Bull stiffened and cautiously opened one
eye. A large grizzly bear stood over him. Sitting
Bull could now smell the bear's strong odor,
which nearly made him cough. But obedient to
the bird's warning, he closed his eyes and lay very
still.

The bear smelled him and nudged him with
his paw, then ambled off, as bears will if they find

the object lifeless. Sitting Bull was saved. He jumped up and looked about for the bird that had saved his life. There it was, perched on a branch. Sitting Bull spoke to the bird, thanked it for its help, and promised that henceforth he would consider the bird his relative and praise it everywhere. On the way back to camp, Sitting Bull made up a chant in honor of the bird that had saved his life. Later, when he danced in the war dances, he sang several more chants, made in honor of the Bird People.

Up to this time, Sitting Bull had not considered himself a singer. There were several men in the camp who sang much better than he. But with the inspiration given him by his vision, Sitting Bull began to practice singing in the evenings inside his father's tipi. It was quite customary for young men, and adults too, to practice evenings indoors, beating a drum or playing the flute or singing. Soon people in camp began to comment that he had a pleasing voice, and asked him to sing at councils and other gatherings. Sitting Bull was sure, of course, that he was successful because the Bird People were favoring him.

With the added power of a vision, a man had confidence to face any enemy as well as the largest buffalo. The Sioux faced enemies periodically. Sometimes they did the attacking, and sometimes they were attacked. But a Sioux hunter faced buffalo regularly.

3

THE BUFFALO IN SIOUX LIFE

HUNTING BUFFALO was the most exciting of all occupations for the Sioux men. They prepared themselves for this from childhood. They practiced and perfected horseback riding on different buffalo ponies. They trained their ponies. They observed buffaloes singly and in herds to learn how these formidable beasts behaved.

The number of buffalo on the plains has been estimated at an astronomical figure of over twelve-million head. An eyewitness in the early part of the eighteenth century described one herd that covered many miles—as far as his eyes could see. It contained about a half a million head, milling about in clouds of insects and dust in the summer heat.

Another traveler reported that at this time the buffalo wandered toward low swampy places, where they cooled off. The leader of the herd usually plowed into the ground with his horns in search of cool, moist layers. As the wallow filled with water, the bull threw himself in, thrashing around with his horns and shoulders to enlarge the hole and to sink deeper into the cooling mud. After a while, cooled and, for the moment, free of the pesty insects, the bull would get up and shake himself. The mud remained plastered to his coat for a time. Later, when it dried, he rubbed it off. Another bull now took the leader's place in the mudhole. Catlin tells of a long line-up of bulls he once witnessed near such a wallow, each awaiting his turn to cool off.

A herd of buffalo on the move is a terrifying force. It permits no obstacle to stand in its way. If its leader has squeezed through an opening, the rest will follow, trampling and crushing everything in their path. The easiest way to kill buffalo was to direct the herd toward a cliff. As the leaders reached the brink, they had no way to turn back, and went over the cliff. The rest of the herd also pressed forward. Another way to kill them was to set fire to the grass all around a buffalo herd and to shoot the poor terrified beasts as they frantically milled about in circles or plunged into the burning barrier, unable to escape. Still another method was to drive the buffalo into a stockade and shoot the animals as they entered.

The Sioux and other Plains Indians trained their ponies for buffalo hunts, as well as for war. These little horses were about a third the size of a buffalo. They were trained to dash into a herd from the rear. The Sioux were superb riders, but at first they did not know the proper care of their animals. In the early days the horse death rate must have been very high.

The hunters, stripped to their breechcloths and moccasins, used no saddles. A man hung his whip from his wrist to be used in case his horse needed goading—although most ponies did not. A trained horse usually needed little guidance, so the rein

hung loosely. Each hunter held his bow in his left
hand, and in his right he held several arrows.
Most hunters left their quiverful of arrows behind. A hunter directed his horse toward the buffalo he had selected in the herd. The pony
approached the buffalo from the right. It knew
just how close to come to the buffalo before veer-
ing away. The rider had enough time to shoot his
arrow to the left of the buffalo's heart. If his first
arrow went off the mark, he had time for another

arrow or two in quick succession, before the pony carried him away. The buffalo might fall in its tracks, it might continue running for a while before it dropped, or it might turn and attack. If attacked, pony and rider had to make a quick getaway.

The ease with which the practiced Sioux hunters went after the buffalo made it seem as though hunting was easy. It was not. Danger followed every hunter at all times. No records were kept of mishaps, but there must have been many. If a hunter fell from his pony, rolled over in the grass away from the stampeding herd, and came out alive, with just a mouthful of dirt, he was lucky indeed. His friends might laugh at him, but they were just as happy that he was alive. A hunter kept a long line trailing behind him during a hunt. If a rider was unseated, he grabbed this thong to keep a hold on his frightened pony.

White men who hunted buffalo reported that during a hunt they were so absorbed in the business at hand that they had no time to think of danger. They acted automatically. Many men, who might otherwise have been less brave, were carried away by the action and chase, and showed unusual courage in the face of danger. Each hunter at one time or another witnessed some frightful accident, where a man was trampled by the pressing herd or gored to death by an enraged bull.

The best buffalo skins for robes were obtained in winter, when the buffalo fur was thick and the hair long. The Sioux knew how to use snowshoes and could follow the buffalo. Since the snow tended to pile up in low places, the buffalo often got bogged down, and were easily killed. Some hunters dressed in wolfskins to deceive the buffalo, which had no fear of wolves. This enabled the hunters to steal close to a buffalo herd and then shoot.

As their skill in buffalo hunting and horsemanship grew, the Indians of the Dakotas began to organize large buffalo hunts on the plains. Several villages camped together. The police chiefs of all the camps sent out scouts to look for herds. It sometimes took weeks to locate a herd. But the Sioux had pemmican, and used the time of waiting to visit among relatives and friends and to feast. Such a camp, waiting hopefully for a large herd, was always a gay place, full of laughter, singing, beating of drums, dancing, and games. But when a herd was sighted, very strict discipline set in. No one left camp without permission —if at all. The police of each village were in charge, and saw to it that no hunter went out alone. Everyone obeyed these rules.

When they moved camp, it was hard work. They had to load tipi covers, children, horses, dogs, and the many other possessions that made up a Sioux household. Yet the women managed to break up camp very swiftly and to establish themselves in a new place just as fast. They made an ingenious sled, called a travois (tra-voy), out of two tipi poles. They crossed the poles over a horse's head, and let the other ends of the poles drag on the ground. Midway up, a woman looped thongs across the poles, forming a loose net for bundles.

In the old days, when the Sioux lived near lakes in Minnesota and Wisconsin, they built canoes like other lake dwellers. But once they moved to the plains, the Sioux men had little use for boats. When a warrior had to cross a river, he either looked for a shallow place to ford, or crossed on horseback. If the water was turbulent and he lost his seat, a man held onto the rein and trusted his horse to swim across. The Sioux women, however, had baggage to consider in crossing rivers, so they built their own boats, bullboats, for crossing bodies of water. The bullboat was bucket-shaped, and made of a scraped buffalo skin, pulled over a rounded wooden frame and sewed with sinew. The paddles the women used were crude pieces of wood. But the bullboats floated them and the children and the old people—and occasionally even a warrior—safely across.

En route to a buffalo hunt the chiefs of all the villages were always in front, the warriors with them, keeping watch. Behind them came the

women on horseback, their household goods and tipi covers piled on the travois. Babies were laced into their cradles, and the mothers tied the cradles on their saddles or to their backs. Younger children doubled up behind the women. If a herd was sighted, each hunter dashed ahead, leaving his family to catch up when the hunt was over.

Whether several villages were hunting together, or whether only a few men were dashing after a herd of buffalo, there was always an old man who prayed for them. The old man sat quietly away from the general uproar and excitement of the stamping herd. He was praying, or as the Sioux say, sending his voice to the spirits above, so the powers would send success to the hunters and keep them unharmed.

At the end of the hunt the old man pointed the stem of his pipe toward the six directions—north, south, east, west, up, and down. He let pinches of tobacco float upward toward Wakan Tanka, as he prayed, "O Wakan Tanka, you have taught us your will through a four-legged one, so that your people may walk the sacred path, and that our children and our children's children will be blessed. I am offering this pipe to you, for you are always first. Next, I shall offer this pipe to Ta-tanka, the buffalo. May our four-legged friends remain numerous in their paths, held up by Mother Earth."

There was a ceremonial butchering of a buffalo cow, with more prayers and thanks, before the people began to feast.

"Buffalo meat is of a delicious flavor, resembling our fat beef," wrote a visitor to the Sioux country over a hundred years ago. Today we find that buffalo meat is rather tough as compared with the corn-fed beef to which we are accustomed. The meat has a peculiar gamy flavor. People today get buffalo meat from buffalo preserves, and most say they prefer it ground into hamburgers. Buffalo steak, even when skillfully broiled, takes strong teeth and much chewing.

As soon as a few buffalo were killed, and after the proper prayers were said, the Sioux women filled buffalo-horn cups full of the warm, nourishing buffalo blood, and gave it to the children to drink. They took out the whole buffalo stomach, threw hot stones inside it, which brought the contents to a boil, and had a feast. We know today that its contents of vegetable matter were full of vitamins. Later the hunters enjoyed broiled buffalo steaks for their evening meal.

Pemmican, or the pounded and dried buffalo meat, must have been a life-saving discovery for the Plains Indians. For many days after each hunt the meat racks outside the tipis bent under the weight of drying buffalo meat. The women pulled the slices of meat down and pounded them as they were drying. When the meat was thoroughly dry, they pounded berries and some bear fat into it and stuffed it into huge containers made of skins, called parfleches, where the meat would keep for a long time.

The Sioux usually had ample food. The supply of buffalo seemed inexhaustible in those golden days, although the hunters sometimes had to wander far from camp to find it. The Sioux, together with the other Plains Indians, believed that the buffalo spirits sent out the buffalo to serve their needs. Yet they must have known starvation. The prayers of the Sioux were full of the repetition, "Give us ample food, so the people may live."

In addition, the Dakota also learned to utilize the buffalo for each of their daily needs. Next in importance to meat was the use of the warm, heavy buffalo robes. These seemed a direct answer to their prayers for protection against cold. After a buffalo hunt, the skins were rolled up carefully, to await the time when the women would be through with the meat drying and when the camp would remain in one place for some time. The old women of each camp worked together on these robes, helping each other to stretch the skins, peg them, and clean them. It was a long drawn-out process. Every bit of the inside of the hide had to be rubbed with a paste made up of buffalo brains. With a bone scraper, the women scraped the hide till it was clean. They shook, washed, rubbed, dried, and combed the fur.

The only other time a buffalo skin was ever

washed, it has been said, was when the buffalo cow licked its calf's coat clean right after birth. Thereafter, for the rest of its life, a buffalo only got wet when it took a mud bath during the summer heat or when it got rained or snowed on. Nor would the robe get washed again after it had an owner—unless its wearer was caught in rain or snowfall.

The last process in tanning was to drape the skin over a wooden frame and place it over a small fire. The smoke from the fire penetrated it through and through, leaving the robe soft and flexible. To decorate a robe was a woman's last and most pleasant duty. She either embroidered the inside with porcupine-quill designs, or painted it with geometric figures in earth colors. Each woman had her own ideas about these designs. They were all tastefully laid out. Indian women had great talent in carrying out these designs.

A robe had many, many uses. It was worn as a wrap-around blanket. It was used as bedding and as a cover. Spread out in the center of a tipi, it made an excellent rug for games. It could also be folded for a comfortable, soft seat. Robes made the finest gifts. They were in demand in trade among the Indians themselves, and between Indians and non-Indians.

A rather unique use of a robe was first made by a Sioux named Lone Dog. Lone Dog painted a historic record on a buffalo robe. This record and several others painted on robes are still in existence. They were called winter counts. The Sioux counted the years in winters. A man, they said, was so many winters old. Lone Dog's winter-count record covered the years of 1800 to 1881. He put down a memorable event for each year. Lone Dog used illustrations that were equivalent to ideographs. He paid special attention to wars and raids, since this was of uppermost interest to the Sioux men. Many years later several Plains Indians were asked to "read" this winter count. They were able to tell the events and the years in which they took place. One man said, pointing to an event inscribed on the robe, "I was born in that year."

Some of Lone Dog's winter counts are:

1801–2 Many die of smallpox.

1802–3 A Dakota stole horses with horseshoes. (From white men.)

1806–7 Many eagles killed.

1811–12 Twenty-seven Mandan surrounded and killed by Dakota.

1828–9 A white man, Chaldron, built a house.

1833–4 The stars fell. (This was the great meteoric shower, observed by astronomers the world over, which took place on November 12.)

1865–6 General Maynadier made peace with the Oglala and the Brulé Sioux.

1876–7 Horses taken by United States government. (It is of interest that Lone Dog did not think the Custer battle important enough to record here.)

1877–8 A man ran a bayonet into Crazy Horse. (Crazy Horse was a famous Oglala chief.)

The word *tipi* is of Sioux origin and means dwelling. *Ti* means dwelling, and *pi*, used for. To make durable tipi covers, buffalo skins had to be scraped clean on both sides. Then the skins were smoked thoroughly. It has been said in praise of the Sioux tanners that the thick, stiff tipi cover lasted a lifetime. It took between five and twenty

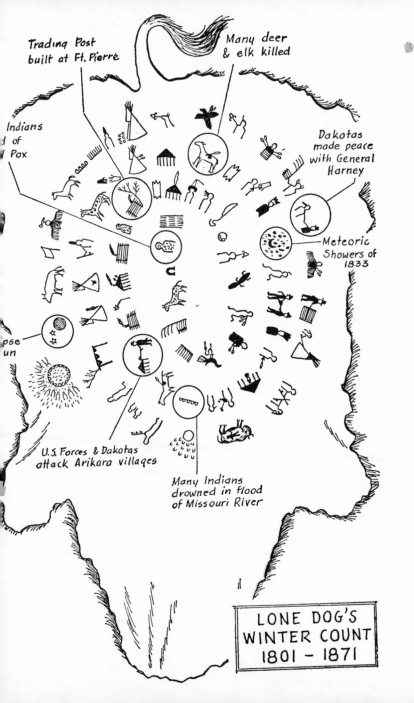

Trading Post
built at Ft. Pierre

Many deer
& elk killed

Indians
d of
Pox

Dakotas
made peace
with General
Harney

Meteoric
Showers of
1833

pse
un

U.S. Forces & Dakotas
attack Arikara villages

Many Indians
drowned in flood
of Missouri River

LONE DOG'S
WINTER COUNT
1801 - 1871

buffalo skins to a tipi, depending of course on the size of the tipi a woman wanted. The skins were sewed together with wet sinew. When it dried, the seams fitted so tightly that they were water-proof.

In setting up a tipi, two or three women un-folded the tipi cover and laid it on the ground. They tied a top corner and a bottom corner to a pole—the setting pole. They pushed the rest of the poles, which were tied together at the top, through the smoke hole, the opening at the top of the tipi. They then lifted up the poles, spread them in a circle, and fitted them into the ground. Then they stretched and tied the tipi cover over the poles. In cold weather the tipi cover was firmly pressed to the ground. Rocks and earth, piled over the edge, kept the wind from blowing in and kept rain and snow out. In summer the tipi cover was rolled up a few feet off the ground to let the breeze cool the tipi and yet maintain a good shade overhead.

In warm weather the women made small fires outside the tipi, and heated stones for boiling food.

These were put inside containers filled with water to bring the contents to a boil. In cool weather they built a small fire inside the tipi for cooking and warmth. A camp after dark, with small fires burning inside each tipi, looked very gay and homey. The little fires, reflecting through the skins, looked pink, and the people, moving near the fires inside the tipis, filled them with dancing shadows. Each woman decorated the outside of her tipi with designs her husband favored, of buffalo or birds or just geometric figures. People knew by the designs to whom a tipi belonged.

Sometimes there was a need for a large lodge in which to hold a council or in which to entertain visitors. Then several women dismantled their tipis and tied the covers together to make a very large lodge.

The poles for a tipi were about twenty-five feet long, tapering from about a four-inch thickness at the bottom to about one inch at the top. For a tipi pole, the Sioux chose a straight young tree— it might be a lodgepole pine, a cedar, or a spruce. The poles often came from as far away as the

Black Hills. Once acquired, the dozen or more poles for a tipi lasted a long time.

Along the walls inside the tipis the women arranged their household goods and bedrolls. They stored most of the household goods in the large buffalo-hide containers called parfleches. The parfleche was between two and three feet long. Its ends folded over like those of an envelope, and it was strong and safe for big and small articles. It was also an excellent container in which to pack pemmican to be transported on the travois. The Plains women made mats occasionally, but they did not make baskets, so each household needed several parfleches.

The buffalo hide for a parfleche was scraped carefully on both sides and tanned. Then the housewife punched holes in the ends and attached thongs. After she filled a parfleche, she folded and tied the sides together. The contents in a parfleche were safe even on a bumpy travois. A parfleche was very practical for the Sioux, since it was always packed and tied ready for moving.

As usual with people who liked to see beautiful things about them, the Sioux women spent considerable effort in decorating their parfleches. They painted geometric designs in different earth colors—green, red, blue, and yellow. The geometric designs were the specialty of women, as was working with porcupine quills. Whenever there were figures painted on a hide, it was usually the work of men. After the skin for a parfleche was cut, the holes punched, and thongs attached to them for tying, the man of the house might turn from the arrows he was making or the pipe bowl he was chipping, and paint a design on a parfleche.

Sinew, like porcupine quills, was always in a woman's workbag. She pulled the strips of sinew from the leg and thigh muscles of the buffalo. Then she soaked the strips and pulled them apart to make the thread she needed for seams. Men also needed sinew for their bows and arrows. First they glued the arrows together with a glue made by boiling buffalo hoofs. Then they reinforced them with the sinew. A man twisted his bowstring out of sinew, and often reinforced the back of the bow with sinew.

Shields, so important in warfare, were also made from the skin of a buffalo—the skin of the neck. Sometimes young men made shields for themselves; sometimes they asked an old man, a craftsman in leather, to make a shield for them. The skin for a shield was cut twice the size it would be when finished. The man who made the shield first dug a hole two or three feet deep. The hole was as large in diameter as the shield would eventually be. He built a fire in the hole. After the fire had been reduced to smoking coals, he put the hide over it, and pegged it around the hole. His friends came to watch, to help a little, and to sing songs and dance, so the shield would gain extra power.

As the skin for the shield warmed, the man spread glue over it. The glue helped make the skin even stiffer as it shrank in the heat. As the skin shrank, it pulled against the pegs, and the men moved the pegs nearer to the edge of the hole.

When the shrinking was finished and the hide had cooled, the shield had shrunk to half its original size, and was now twice as thick. The man smoothed the edges. The shield was now ready for decoration and for a few handsome eagle feathers to set it off. The decorations were painted onto the outer surface, and were marks or symbols that the owner held sacred.

A shield against bows and arrows was a most essential protection for a warrior. He carried it over his left arm and moved it swiftly against flying arrows. The surface was slightly concave. Flying arrows glanced off the thick, stiff shield, thus saving many a warrior's life.

A shield used in battle was treated with respect. It had absorbed additional strength in victory as well as through the blessings and prayers medicine men bestowed upon the warriors before a battle. A shield must never touch the ground when not in use. It hung in a safe buckskin cover on a special pole in or outside the tipi. A battle-scarred shield was the pride of its owner and was feared by friend and foe alike.

No dance or festival was possible without a few drums, rattles, whistles, flutes, and other noise-makers. The drumheads and rattles were of buffalo skin too. After a drum had been used in ceremonies, it also became sacred, for it was round like the earth and the heavens, and so carried in it the sacred powers of both. The sound of the drum was like the heartbeat of its people or like the voice of Wakan Tanka. That was why the drum beat stirred and moved the dancers.

A drum used in ceremonies was treated with care. When not in use, it was covered with a soft buckskin and kept in the far end of a tipi—which the Sioux considered a place of honor. Some drums were merely pieces of hide stretched over hoops. The hide was stretched while wet. As it dried, it shrank and remained taut over the hoop. Other drums, especially those used in ceremonies, had two heads that had been stretched over a piece of wood, which had been hollowed out. The sound of these drums carried quite far.

Drumsticks were made of sticks covered at one end with a wad of soft buckskin. Rattles, used by men in dances to emphasize rhythm and also as drumsticks, were made of buffalo hide. While still wet, the hide was sewed on a wooden handle. A man put a few pebbles or seeds into the hide before it was sewed together. When they dried, these buffalo-hide rattles were as stiff as rattles made of gourds, and could last forever.

The horns and bones of the buffalo were also used. Men worked the stiff horns into all sorts of household articles and toys. They chipped and scraped buffalo horns into cups and dishes. They split them into odd-shaped containers for food and paints. From horns they made tops and other toys for their children. When guns came to the Sioux, horns proved to be excellent waterproof containers for gunpowder.

Men saved the buffalo's ribs to make sleds for their children. They took advantage of the natural, curved shape of four to six buffalo ribs, and tied a piece of buffalo hide across this frame made of ribs. This was the youngster's seat. Straddling his little sled, a youngster could slide downhill, steadying himself with heavy thongs made of buf-

falo hide, which his father had tied to the front of the sled. When there was no snow, the children used the sled for a rocker or mounted it in their games as though it were a pony.

Buffalo bones were sharpened and used as awls in sewing and for etching designs. When the end of a bone was softened by chewing, it became a brush for painting. The buffalo's shoulder blades were used as digging tools.

The stomach of the buffalo, after its contents had been enjoyed by the entire family, was scraped clean and washed. It made an excellent container for carrying and storing water. Since the Sioux did not make clay pottery, they used these containers for cooking too.

Even the tail of the buffalo was used—as a fly swatter.

A Sioux housewife, glancing about her home, was grateful to the buffalo for everything inside her comfortable tipi—for the pile of buffalo robes, the parfleches bulging with good pemmican, the covered drums and rattles, the extra pairs of moccasin soles in her sewing box, and for the shield that stood guard outside the tipi. She must have looked up at the sky and sun and offered a prayer of thanks to Wakan Tanka for being so generous to the People of the Dakota.

4

RAIDS, COUPS, AND SCALPS

As THE SIOUX pushed out onto the plains, they found other groups of Indians living there, and promptly began warring with them. Some of these groups spoke dialects similar to the Siouan language, and so must have been related to the Sioux in the past. This did not always stop the Dakota. They cared only for their own close kin. No one in camp ever went hungry if any hunter had food. But outsiders received little consideration. When the Sioux met the Indians who had settled along the Missouri, they drove them from their homes.

These wars and raids were different, of course, from the wars the Sioux were to face later against the white men. Against white men the Sioux fought for their very lives—for their lands and the buffalo on them.

In the early days young men were anxious for action and fame. They found both in a war or in a raid—if they survived. Most of them did survive. With the proper prayers, and fortified by the power they knew they had from a vision, these young men ventured forth, confident that they would not only survive, but would return to their camp with coups and scalps.

Each warrior kept strict count of his deeds of glory—his coups. To count coup (koo) meant to strike an enemy. The word came from the French and Latin. While recounting their exploits during a dance, warriors struck a post to mark each deed. The French named it *coup*, or blow, and the name stuck. Each man carried his little feathered coup stick to battle with him for this purpose.

There were several grades of coups. The first was to touch an enemy during a battle. That called for greater courage than shooting him with an

WARRIOR'S RECORDS

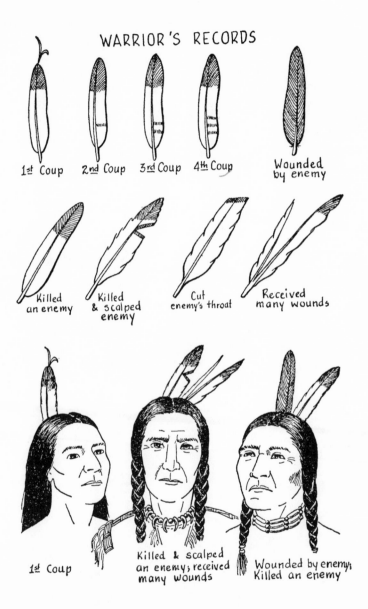

1st Coup 2nd Coup 3rd Coup 4th Coup Wounded by enemy

Killed an enemy Killed & scalped enemy Cut enemy's throat Received many wounds

1st Coup

Killed & scalped an enemy; received many wounds

Wounded by enemy; Killed an enemy

arrow or a gun and touching him afterward. The first man who touched a living enemy counted a "first coup." Three other men could touch the same enemy and count coup. These were second coups. Several warriors could also count first and second coups on a slain enemy, if the dead man was surrounded by his own warriors.

The third grade of coup was to cut loose a horse within the enemy camp. All warriors valued their specially trained mounts. A warrior often slept with his horse's rein tied inside the tipi. So if anyone wanted to steal the horse, the owner would be awakened by the pull on the rope. To cut loose such a horse required courage, and so counted as a coup.

A youth who had not counted coup had not attained manhood. No girl would marry him. He had to keep quiet at council meetings. During dances each warrior got up and, as he danced, chanted aloud his feats of bravery. Even old men got up to dance and recite the deeds they had performed many years before. The audience shouted their approval of these deeds just as loudly, even though everyone had already heard them recited many, many times. Having nothing to boast of, the young men hid behind the backs of others, dreaming of the day when they, too, would be able to get up and recite their coups, and have the men shout approval and the women sing out in peculiar high-pitched voices.

Among the Sioux, successful warriors planned the wars and raids. A warrior had several experienced scouts, who reported to him regularly about what was taking place on the nearby plains. They may have seen a party of Indians, with many horses, moving camp. The scouts reported on the number of people in the camp and the number of warriors. They needed horses for the next buffalo hunt. This would be a good way to get them.

A war chief usually led a large band. He was a man who had counted coup many times and who had many successful raids to his credit. He was known to be careful of his men. His last war party captured many horses, and all the men returned safely home. The war chief knew that young men would be glad to volunteer and go along with him

A messenger with a peace pipe came to invite these men to the war chief's tipi. The messenger usually entered the tipi of a warrior and offered him the calumet to smoke in the name of the war chief. The warrior then knew that a raid was planned. After the messenger sat down and lit the pipe, the warrior took a few puffs. This meant that he was ready to go.

The planning of the raid, the setting of the time, the direction in which they would travel, and other details were discussed in the meetings that followed the invitation. The war chief usually invited to these councils an old man—a medicine man—who had special powers. After prayers and after consulting the sacred bundle in his possession, the wise man could foretell the successful outcome of the expedition that the war chief was organizing.

A younger brother or nephew of a warrior was often taken along to receive extra training. He usually remained in the background and performed small services for the warriors, tending their mounts, carrying water, and helping with meals. If the raid was successful, he might get a horse and even count coup.

When the raiding party came near the enemy camp, they rested for the day. The men took off any extra clothing and moccasins they carried with them and hid them in a safe place—to be reclaimed later. No fire was lit that night. The men might chew on some pemmican, or they might wish to fast, so the spirits would favor them the next day.

At dawn the men painted themselves to frighten the enemy, and crept into their camp. At a signal, the warriors yelled their war whoops and bore down on the enemy. The raid and the counting of coups were accomplished swiftly.

Having rounded up the enemy's horses, the warriors raced for home. If there were more men in the enemy camp, the raiders were sure to be pursued. If the raiders felt they were going to be overtaken, they might let the newly captured horses go. If their war chief felt they should fight it out with the enemy, they might make a stand.

Later, the enemy would find out who the

raiders were and plan a counter attack to recover their horses and perhaps steal some in turn. The raiders' camp might be attacked at dawn, and then, not only warriors, but everyone else in camp —including women and children—might be killed. Young warriors expected to die in battle, but too often they brought death and destruction to their own people.

The Sioux were not always the initiators of wars and raids. Other groups on the plains trespassed on lands the Sioux claimed as theirs. The Sioux were always ready to fight such intruders. If the intruders were numerous, many Sioux camps might unite against the common enemy.

At best, the wars and raids were on a small scale, with little destruction to life and property. Raids in which several men were killed were rare in the early days. They became more frequent when guns were introduced by white traders and trappers.

In the 1830's Catlin witnessed a Sioux attack on their traditional enemies, the Mandan Indians, who were farmers and lived in permanent villages

the Missouri River. By that time the Man-
had been reduced through disease to a very
small group. Being so few, the men no longer
dared to go too far from their villages to hunt
buffalo. Instead, they held buffalo dances. The
belief of all Indians was that through strenuous
dancing, imitating the steps and movements of
buffalo, and with the constant beating of the
drum, the spirits would bring enough buffalo di-
rectly to them. Accordingly, these Mandan hunters had danced continuously for two weeks, and
they were exhausted. One of their scouts rushed
into camp, saying that he had just received a signal from another scout far away that a herd of
buffalo had been sighted in a nearby valley. The
Mandan drums stopped. Men rushed to their
horses, grabbed a few arrows, and, threading their
bows en route, dashed off in high hopes.

In high hopes, too, the village chiefs took out
the last of the dried meat, which the women had
carefully saved. The women made fires. They
quickly cooked the meat, and everyone in the

camp—the old men, the women, and the children —ate their fill for the first time in many weeks. They had barely finished when mourning cries broke out. Several horses raced in with their dead masters tied to their backs. Soon several wounded hunters came limping into the camp.

An attack had been carefully planned by a raiding party of Sioux. They heard the drumming for the buffalo dance and knew that the Mandan were starving. The Sioux captured one Mandan scout, then gave false signals with the buffalo robe to the other scouts, telling them that there was a large herd of buffalo nearby. A few Sioux warriors, wearing buffalo robes, crouched in the valley, so that it appeared from a distance as though buffalo really were grazing. As the hungry Mandan hunters headed for the valley, the Sioux were ready to count coups.

In Catlin's report eight Mandan were killed that day. On such a large number of dead, every Sioux warrior in the party must have counted coup several times. At least eight Sioux warriors car-

ried Mandan scalps triumphantly back with them, to add to their glory and to boast about in loud voices at the next war dance.

It did not take great skill, but it did take courage to take a scalp while surrounded by enemies. Not only the Sioux but all the Plains Indians took scalps at one time or another, but they scalped only a dead enemy. This custom is horrifying to us, for we have been taught to respect the dead and to offer burial even to enemies. The center of the scalp, where the hair grows in a circle, seemed a particularly meaningful spot to the Indians. The Sioux regarded the circle as *wakan*, or sacred, for the sun was round, the moon was round, the stars, their shields, and drums were round. In taking and owning a scalp, a warrior gained his enemy's power.

The way the Sioux took the scalp of a dead enemy was to grasp the hair on a victim's crown with the left hand and, with a sharp knife, to cut the skin around the circle of hair. The size of the skin on a scalp was as large as a man's palm. In addition, the warrior also cut off the rest of the victim's hair. His wife later sewed the scalp and hair in small bunches onto the seams of his shirt and leggings as decoration. This generous display of scalps on a man's shirt boosted his vanity.

There were instances when a Sioux struck an enemy with a war club, and the victim lost consciousness. In the heat of battle, thinking the person dead, the Sioux warrior then proceeded to collect this scalp. Later the victim regained consciousness. He must have found the scalped area bleeding and exceedingly painful, but it was not fatal, and in time the victim recovered, although hair never grew on his scalped crown.

A scalping knife was a part of every warrior's outfit. It was really a knife used for many other purposes besides scalping. In the old days, before white men brought metal knives to the Indians, their knives were made of stone or bone and were quite as sharp as a metal blade. A warrior carried his knife in a sheath in his belt.

The tomahawk was a very valuable addition to the warrior's possessions, and came to the Indians through trade with white men. The tomahawk was of metal, and was shaped like a small ax. Its head was scooped out to make a pipe bowl. The Indians appreciated the tomahawk, because it took the place of several tools. It could be used as an ax, as a war club, as a scalping knife, and as a pipe. The handle, which was also a pipestem, was carefully worked by its owner, and hollowed out with great labor and patience. The way to make this hollow was to burn its center patiently with a heated wire. There were endless artistic variations in designing these handles for pipestems, just as there were in carving long stems for peace pipes and in decorating them with porcupine quills, beads, leather, feathers, and strips of fur.

Once a man had taken a scalp with his knife or tomahawk, it remained in his possession for the rest of his life. After a raid, he dried the scalp carefully and mounted it with sinew on a hoop of wood, so it could be carried on a long stick. On special occasions a chief mounted the scalps he owned on a long pole, which stuck out of the top of his tipi. When a chief did this, it was a signal for lesser chiefs and warriors in the village to display the scalps they owned, so visitors to a village might be treated to a view of all the brave deeds performed by its men. Boys in the village liked to walk about looking at the scalps. Each had been seen in the village ceremonies many times, and a boy knew by the scalps to whom a tipi belonged.

Catlin sketched several scalp dances while he visited the Sioux. He described these dances in detail. The scalp dance was always the last feature of an evening's celebration. These scalp dances lasted for fifteen nights after the men returned from a successful raid. The women carried to the dance all the scalps their men owned. They stood in the center of the dancing area, holding the scalps on poles, while the warriors, who had taken the scalps, danced around them. The warriors were fully armed with bows and arrows, spears, and shields. They leaped and stamped and circled around the scalps. They yelled and aimed their weapons at the scalps, as though they were threatening a living enemy. They made horrible faces and rolled their eyes, as they had done in their most recent battle and victory.

The Sioux tell of one time when there was a long period of peace between them and the Arikara. This came about because of a dream that came to a Dakota holy man. In this vision, the holy man, Matohoshila, found a bag of seed corn and brought it back to camp. His people knew that the corn was precious and that the Arikara farmers would starve without it. They decided to return the corn to the Arikara.

On waking, Matohoshila called the men of the

camp together and told them of his dream. There was no doubt in their minds that the spirits wanted the Dakota to make peace with the Arikara. They immediately began to prepare for the peace ceremony.

Runners were sent to call the Arikara camps and other Sioux camps together. It was to be a very complicated ceremony. Soon people began to stream into Matohoshila's camp, setting up tipis and sweat lodges. Each man who was to take part in the ceremony had to fast and spend some time in the sweat lodge, to purify himself in the smoke of sweet grass, sage, and tobacco. Matohoshila tied a buffalo bladder into a sacred bundle. This bundle became as sacred as a peace pipe. Men prayed with it to Wakan Tanka and to the six directions: north, south, east, west, up, and down. They asked them to watch the ceremony and to rejoice that the two nations would no longer fight each other.

The peace ceremony began with a mock raid. Four Sioux let Arikara warriors capture them and count coup on them—as the Sioux had done to the

Arikara many times in the past wars. After the make-believe battle, the Arikara warriors embraced the four Sioux warriors, as though they were embracing the entire Sioux Nation. The Arikara and Sioux were now as brothers. Each promised never to break the peace.

After this there was a feast, followed by dances and games. The visitors remained at Matohoshila's camp for several days. Families visited in one another's tipis, feasting together, playing games, and dancing.

5

GAMES

EVERY SIOUX looked forward with pleasure to the yearly events of festivals, games, and dances, as did all Indians of the plains. All these activities had ceremonial and religious meanings. It was, therefore, quite natural for people to mix chants and prayers, feasts and sacrifices with their games and dances.

Winning a game had the same meaning as winning a war. The bets collected after a game were similar to getting horses in a raid. A man who won a game was sure that the spirits favored him and that the next raid would be a success for him, too.

Everyone played games and everyone danced,

although some were more active than others. Women and girls danced less than the men. But they were an important audience. The men liked to show off before them, and the women and girls showed their appreciation with high-pitched calls of approval. There were games for the outdoors and games for indoors. The out-of-door games were more active. Because of the size of the tipi, people played indoor games sitting in one place.

To begin with, everyone took part in races. Foot races were ancient games. In the old days the Sioux were proud of being good runners. Later they were proud of having fast horses. Horsemen enjoyed showing off their fast mounts. Any visitor to a camp, who boasted of having a particularly fast pony, found many young men willing to race him, with offers of generous bets. And whenever foot races were held, the young horsemen readily joined in. Some foot races covered a three-mile stretch.

The hoop and pole games were also ancient, and were played by Sioux of all ages. The men rolled saplings into hoops. Two teams of men or boys,

holding spears, lined up. One man rolled the hoop toward the players. As the hoop came within the proper distance, a man thrust his spear through it. Playing hoop and pole games improved a man's marksmanship, and so they were good training for a hunter.

In the winter the men liked to show off their strength and skill in games of snow snake. Although this game was also played by boys and girls and women, the men's game was really more exciting. Each player had a long stick, which he hurled through the snow. The snow snake that traveled farthest won, and everyone present shouted in appreciation for the winner. If a contest took place between opposing teams, bets were placed, and the winner went home with perhaps an extra robe or a horse.

There were also contests in archery among men and among boys. Here, too, people placed bets. As the men competed, there was much talking, shouting, and laughter everywhere. Adults took sides when there were contests in archery among the boys. The best shots received gifts from the audience. The boys spent long hours practicing archery, using cactus plants, pieces of hide, bundles of grass, and even small dead animals as targets. The boy whose arrow went the farthest into the grass bundle had the privilege of throwing the bundle as far as he could, and the other boys had to try and shoot their arrows into it. Sometimes a boy, who was a very good shot, shot an arrow into a hillside. The other boys who were with him tried to hit the hillside with their arrows as close to his as possible.

Young archers also trained in speed. Several boys or young men got eight or ten arrows ready.

At a signal, they shot the arrows into the air at such high speed that before the first one reached the ground, the archer had finished shooting all the arrows in his hand.

Everyone also played ball games. Young men played a game that resembled lacrosse. It was a rough game, and there was no limit to the number of people on a team. The field was very large, and the soft ball, made of buckskin stuffed with hair, was small. People on opposite teams pushed one another, fell on top of each other, and often hit opponents on the head with their rackets. Two friendly camps, playing opposite each other, might end up as bitter enemies, because a game of lacrosse had not turned out well. A return match the following day or at a later date often helped soothe hurt feelings.

Often lacrosse players invited women and girls to play opposite them. But the women were allowed to handle the ball with both hands, while the men used only rackets. With this advantage, the women and girls often won and collected bets. This usually caused banter among the men, but there were no hard feelings, since the members of the opposing team were often their own wives and daughters.

Sometimes Sioux women and girls were asked to play their favorite stick-ball game, while the men watched. Catlin described a women's ball game to which he was invited. The women and girls of the camp divided into two teams. Each woman held two sticks, one in each hand. The

teams took their positions on the field opposite each other. Two balls, tied with heavy thongs about a foot and a half in length, were thrown high into the air by a man who acted as umpire. The balls must not touch the ground. The women ran to the center, trying to catch the balls by balancing them on their sticks. The woman who caught them then threw them to a teammate, who, in turn, caught the balls on her sticks. In this way, the balls passed from one player to the next and to the goal.

The players crowded and pushed, while the men sat around the field, making comments, calling to the players, teasing some of them, and encouraging others.

This game, Catlin reported, lasted several hours. When it was over, the women who scored goals received the bets that had been placed by the men. There were kettles, beads, pieces of cloth, mirrors, buttons, needles and thread.

Indoor games, because they were sedentary, were games between two, four, or six persons. They were mostly guessing games, and each player placed a small bet. A little bundle of sticks contained one odd stick, which might be colored black or red. A player closed his eyes and divided the bundle into two parts. He then offered one of the halves to his opponent. If the odd stick was in the half the opponent chose, he won. It was his turn then to shut his eyes and divide the bundle. Each player kept careful count with pebbles on the number of games he had won. In the end, the person who won the most games collected all the bets.

The moccasin game was the same kind of guessing game. One person put a small piece of bone or a pebble into one of three moccasins. Again small bets were placed. The opponent tried to guess which moccasin held the pebble. There was an interesting variation on this game. If the person guessed right the first time, he lost. But if he guessed wrong, he got another chance to guess— and perhaps win the game.

While adults were playing, the children watched the game or turned to another part of the tipi to spin tops. Children played with them both indoors and outdoors. Their fathers made them tops of bone, of horn and antlers, and of wood.

In this way, long winter evenings, rainy weather, and the time between hunts passed rapidly. Always, of course, the women of the household were kept busy with their cooking, sewing, mending, embroidering, and the care of their children. But when women visited each other, they also played guessing games and the moccasin game, placing small bets as their menfolk did.

6

THE SUN DANCE AND OTHERS

THE SIOUX enjoyed dances as much as they enjoyed games. Through their dances men and women expressed every important happening in their daily lives, their joys and their sorrows. They danced also to please the spirits and, as in the Sun Dance, they danced to insure the coming of the buffalo. Many dances, such as the Bear Dance, were grotesque and clownish, and were intended to amuse the people. Others were intended to arouse pity, and some—the war dances, for example—were intended to terrify. Stamping, leaping, yelling, and singing, with the beating of drums, whistles, rattles, and other noisemakers, were part of each dance.

Since every Sioux man wanted to be conspicuous and well-known, no one held back in expressing himself. They danced, as they warred and played games, in utter freedom and abandon. But the men liked their wives and their daughters to show modesty, so the women's dancing was very quiet, with slow, controlled motions. In some dances the women and girls just stood in the center of the dance lodge, swaying slightly to the rhythm of the drums and rattles, holding their husbands' shields or poles with scalps.

The audience sat, stood, and walked around the dance area. Men and youths, who were not in the dance, and male visitors trouped about, chatting, gossiping, applauding, and shouting at the dancers. In other small groups were women nursing their babies and watching small children who required continuous attention. These mothers, despite their responsibilities, also enjoyed themselves. When a woman had to join in a dance, she found ready neighbors to care for her baby while she was dancing. When gathering together, the Indian women were not very different from a gathering of women in other parts of the world. They gossiped, they exchanged news, they admired each other's clothing, they exchanged opinions on designs, on ways to care for their children and keep them healthy, and on ways of cooking and improving foods.

Everyone carefully watched each dance with intense, lively interest. There were shouts of appreciation if the performers were good and shouts of derision if the performers were bad—or if a boastful warrior was carried away and claimed honors for himself he did not deserve.

The Sioux audience also showed a fine sense of humor, even if the joke was aimed against them. Catlin told of a most unusual dance which he saw at a Sioux camp, and which proved to him that the Sioux were the best of audiences. He was among a large gathering of Sioux near a trading post. The Sioux had come to trade, and had set themselves up in several hundred tipis, so it was a large audience that watched the groups of dancers from the different camps perform. One camp had finished and its dancers had retired, when a tall, statuesque woman stepped forward alone into the dancing area to represent her camp. The audience looked at her in quiet surprise. They had expected several dancers.

The woman began to dance, making stately movements in her heavy buffalo robe. After a while, she raised her voice and began to recite the brave things she had done. They were mainly deeds of raids and a detailed recounting of how many horses she had stolen. She then went on to shout that she had also taken scalps. With motions, she showed how she had scalped her enemies. The audience evidently believed her, and shouted encouragement for her to continue.

When the woman finished, everyone seemed delighted with the performance, and one chief stepped into the dancing area and gave the woman an iron kettle and a handsome buckskin for a cradleboard. The dancer handed these articles over to another woman, her attendant. Then she

brushed her loose hair from her face and let th
buffalo robe slip off. The audience burst out
laughing. Before them stood a warrior, dressed
in a fringed buckskin shirt and leggings. Everyone
shouted with glee. They could more readily be-
lieve that a man had done all that the performer
claimed to have done. With stamps, leaps, and
yells, the performer circled about, balancing his
spear and shouting how brave he was, how many
scalps he had taken, how many coups he had
counted, and how many horses he had stolen. The
audience continued to shout encouragement to
him.

When this dance was finished, a man led his
horse over to the dancer and gave it to him; the
trader gave him a gun and some tobacco. An old
man gave the brave warrior a war club. Again the
performer accepted the gifts and handed them
over to the woman attendant, who Catlin now
thought must be his wife.

But the performer did not retire from the field.
Instead, the woman helped him pull off his shirt
and leggings. A young woman, in a beautifully

worked buckskin dress, now stood before the audience. She moved slowly in a dance, as became a modest Sioux maiden. Everyone went wild with delight at being so completely deceived. The people cheered, laughed, and shouted in appreciation. The maiden stopped dancing and stood still, facing the audience. When the noise subsided, the camp chief got up, went into the dancing area, and placed a beautiful eagle feather in the girl's hair. She richly deserved this mark of bravery.

The Dakota usually named their dances for the person, animal, or spirit they intended to honor. There were also dances for a special purpose, such as the Beggar's Dance. This might be danced several times during the year. The dancers were the camp's young men. They dressed up in beautifully embroidered breechcloths and kilts, wore eagle feathers in their hair, and carried spears and rattles. A holy man beat the drum for this dance. The dancers sang in high-pitched voices, and circled around and around, stamping heel and toe. Each sang as loudly as he could, for this dance was an appeal to Wakan Tanka to influence the hearts of the audience to give to the poor. Wakan Tanka was kind to those who cared for the poor.

At the end of the Beggar's Dance the audience gave away robes, horses, and food. This public giving did not embarrass anyone, because everyone expected men to be generous. The greater the warrior, the greater his generosity was supposed to be. That was why the best warriors and the best hunters among the Sioux were usually poor men. They hunted all the time to provide not only for their own families, but for those who were orphaned or who were too old to go after the buffalo.

The Eagle Dance was one of the most precious dances among the Sioux. Sixteen men took part in it, dancing four at a time. Four was considered a lucky number. Each person danced around a pole, which was a spear stuck in the ground. The dancers wore feathers in their hair, and each held an eagle's tail in one hand. They squatted in rows of four, one behind the other. As one row of dancers circled the posts, imitating eagles swooping down, turning, and circling, the second row of dancers moved forward. When the first row of dancers tired, the second row resumed the dance, and the first row moved to the back. After the remaining two rows of dancers had had their turns, the rested first-row dancers were ready to take their turn again.

The Bear Dance, although full of such clowning as the imitation of the waddling of a bear, was also intended to do honor to the bear spirit. Bear meat was very tasty, and bear grease was essential in making pemmican, paints, and ointments for rubbing down babies and everyone else in cold weather. The leader in this dance was usually the camp medicine man. He wore a bearskin and had an eagle feather in his hair. The other dancers wore bear masks. The Bear Dance was celebrated for several days. The Sioux believed that it would make the bear hunt, which usually followed this celebration, very successful.

The Sioux Dog Dance was one of their most exacting dances. It could only be danced by those who had taken scalps from the enemy and who could come forward to boast that they had killed their enemy in battle and swallowed a piece of his heart.

During this dance a dog was killed, and cut up into small pieces and hung on a rack in the center of the field. While everyone was shouting his deeds and making a deafening racket, the dancers came up in pairs to the center of the area. After spitting several times upon the dog's liver and

heart, each caught a piece of meat in his mouth and swallowed it. This was all done without losing a single step in the violent dance. The last two pieces left hanging were carried in the mouths of two dancers and fed to the two drummers—again without anyone's losing a beat.

The Sun Dance was one of the most important and spectacular dances of the Sioux. It has been described by many non-Indian eyewitnesses, who were awed by what they saw. According to what they said and wrote, the Sun Dance was a deeply impressive ceremony of self-torture, held in a specially designed Sun Dance lodge before thousands of assembled Sioux and other Plains Indians. Eventually the United States government stepped in and prohibited these dances, because during the ritual the Sun Dancers tortured themselves. The government also hoped that stopping the Sun Dance would help the Sioux to forget their old ways.

In the language of the Dakota this dance was called Wiwanyag Wachipi, a Dance-of-looking-at-the-sun. Because the sun was the source of light and lived forever, it was like Wakan Tanka. It was also closely associated with success in buffalo hunting and the abundance of buffalo. The Sun Dance was held at the end of the full moon, either in June or July. June in Sioux was the Moon-of-buffalo-fattening. July was the Moon-of-cherries-blackening. The full moon was the time when Wakan Tanka shed its full light upon the entire world.

The origin of the Sun Dance was told in a Sioux legend. This legend was written down by a Sioux chief, named Black Elk, who was a remarkable man and thinker. He gave the credit for bringing the Sun Dance to the people to an ancient man named Kablaya. Kablaya worried that the people were growing careless in observing their religious ceremonies. They had abandoned the practices that White Buffalo Cow Maiden had told them to follow when she gave them the calumet. Because of this, men were losing their strength.

Kablaya went in search of a vision to guide him in reforming his people. Up on a mountaintop,

Wakan Tanka came to him in a dream, and instructed Kablaya in the ritual to follow in the Dance-of-looking-at-the-sun, which would restore his people's strength. Kablaya returned from his quest and set about to organize a Sun Dance, in which the dancers would offer their bodies and souls to Wakan Tanka, so the people could regain their strength and live happily. Thereafter, the details for these preparations were observed in all Sun Dances.

Many things had to be prepared for this ceremony. Some of the men cut out several circular pieces of rawhide and painted them. One circle was painted red like the sun. Other circles, painted blue, represented the moon, the stars, and the sky. One piece was cut into a five-pointed star, the Morning Star. This star was important, because it stood between darkness and light. It was like man's knowledge, lighting up the darkness of ignorance. Another circle represented mother and grandmother earth, from which all beings sprang. The last circle represented the buffalo, for without the buffalo, men could not live.

Kablaya, in the meantime, practiced sacred chants, which he taught to the dancers. The few words of each chant he made up were very simple. Chants were always simple and repetitious, for the words and singing had to be perfect and had to be memorized.

One chant, for example, was:

> They say the buffalo herd is coming.
> It is here now.
> The blessing will come to us.
> It is with us now.

These simple chants had magic in them. In the Indians' belief if one wished for something and prayed for it and said it had happened, it *would* happen.

Each chant ended with a chorus, which was also repeated several times, "Wakan Tanka have mercy on us that our people may live." Each chorus ended with whistling. The whistle was made of an eagle bone—the voice of Spotted

Eagle, which was the same as the voice of Wakan Tanka.

There had to be a tree in the center of the Sun Dance lodge. The center of the lodge during a ceremony was the same as the center of the earth. The tree then united the earth and the sky. This tree had to be a rustling cottonwood, which grew along riverbanks. A cottonwood was favored, because its heart-shaped leaves resembled the shape of a tipi. In the beliefs of the Sioux, a tree was also a being with a soul. In their chants they called it a "standing person."

Before the ceremony began, the Sioux organized a party to capture and cut down the tree. This party was organized just like a war party, with the same precautions, secrecy, fasting, and prayers. First, as in a war party, scouts went out to look for the tree. When they found one of the right height, they immediately returned to camp with the news.

As was the custom in questioning scouts who returned from a mission, Kablaya, with great solemnity and formality, made the men smoke the pipe first. He then spoke to them to make sure that their minds would be as straight as the hole that ran through the stem of the pipe, and that their tongues would not be forked with untruth. "You have found a tree that will be of great benefit to the people. Tell us rightfully what you have found."

The scouts reported how far they had gone to look for the right trees, or as they said, "for the sacred standing people," and why they had selected this particular tree.

After making their report, the scouts painted themselves black as if for war, and together with Kablaya, who carried the sacred pipe, went over to the tree. In silence, the rest of the camp followed the war party, and stopped some distance away.

Kablaya addressed the tree in a loud, clear voice, and his words had the sound of poetry. "O, rustling cottonwood," he said, "you have been chosen. You are about to go to the center of the people's sacred lodge. There you will represent all your standing people and do honor to Wakan Tanka. You are a kind and handsome tree. Upon you, winged people have rested and raised their families. From the tip of your tall branches down to your roots, the winged and four-legged peoples have made their homes. When you stand in our lodge you will link Mother Earth with the Heavens. The weak will lean upon you. You will support all our people."

Five men were selected to cut the tree down—a chief and four warriors. They did a war dance around the tree first. Since cutting down the sacred tree was like counting coup in wartime, each man recited his previous war deeds before striking the tree. The first to strike was the chief. As the fifth man struck the tree the last blow that felled it, men in the crowd rushed forward, so the tree would not touch the ground but would fall into their arms.

Six men carried the tree to camp. On the way, for good luck, they stopped four times. At the last stop, just before entering camp, they all howled like coyotes. Warriors usually did this when they reached their villages after a victory. The men carefully laid the tree on poles inside the Sun Dance lodge. From the beginning to the end of the Sun Dance, the tree was treated with great respect. No one was permitted to step over it. It was considered impolite to step over the legs of a person resting inside a tipi, and the same politeness was observed here.

All the men now retired to the sweat lodge for a final purification. All the things that were to be used in the Sun Dance, including the sacred circles the men had painted, the drum and rattles, the sacred pipe, and even the robes, leather thongs, screwers, and buffalo skulls the men were to use in the ceremony, were held over the smoke to be purified.

And once again, after sprinkling tobacco over the fire, Kablaya prayed to Wakan Tanka, to Mother Earth, and to the remaining four directions.

From the sweat lodge, the men went into the dance lodge to plant the tree in the center. Again, they danced around the tree. A buckskin bag, filled with fat, was attached to the tree, so that the earth would be fat and plentiful. Twenty-eight poles were placed into the ground, to act as supports for the walls of the lodge. Twenty-eight was also a sacred number, because the life of each moon was twenty-eight days.

The men again retired to the sweat lodge for final arrangements. Those who were to dance in the Sun Dance were to be selected, as well as one woman, who would represent the ancient White Buffalo Cow Maiden. Being a woman, she was not allowed to enter the sweat lodge, but remained standing outside the lodge after the men had entered it.

After another prayer to Wakan Tanka, Kablaya said that he wished to endure great pain in behalf of his people. In tears and suffering he offered the pipe and sent his voice to Wakan Tanka, so the people might live. Kablaya then announced that he would attach four thongs to his body and let his flesh be torn. Since the flesh represented ignorance, Kablaya would also tear away the people's ignorance when he tore his own flesh.

A second man offered himself for the Sun Dance, saying he would attach himself to the four powers of the world. This meant that he would be tied with thongs to four posts. A third man said he would bear four of his closest relatives—the ancient buffalo. This man intended to dance with four buffalo skulls attached to his body. Still another promised twelve pieces of his flesh to lay at the foot of the sacred standing person. One man promised one piece of flesh. The woman, too, offered one piece of her flesh.

After purification, the dancers were not permitted to touch their bodies. Each had a helper, who carried his robe and dance equipment for him. Each dancer also carried a little stick, with which he was permitted to touch his body.

The dance began at dawn. The people had already assembled and sat around the dance lodge, waiting. Kablaya led the procession of dancers from the sweat lodge. White Buffalo Cow Maiden carried the sacred pipe. All the dancers were chanting and crying, "Wakan Tanka, be merciful to me that my people may live. It is for this that

I am sacrificing myself." People in the audience repeated the cry.

Kablaya stepped up to the altar that had been erected inside the lodge, with a buffalo skull on it and a small fire built next to it. He placed over the flame the knife to be used in the dance, and lit a small bundle of sage.

> I give grass to the buffalo,
> for the people to see
> that they may live.

He stuffed sage into the sockets of the buffalo skull and tied a small pouch of tobacco on one of its horns. The sun rose, and Kablaya turned to the east, saying, "The light of Wakan Tanka is upon my people."

The drum began to beat. As its tempo increased, two men rushed up to Kablaya. They threw him roughly on the ground. As one man pulled the skin on his chest, the other pierced it in two places and put in two pegs with long thongs. They tied the ends of the thongs to the sacred tree.

With face raised to the sun, Kablaya continued chanting. He moved around and around the sacred tree, pulling at the thongs. His pierced skin was bleeding. The thongs tightened till the pegs tore his body, leaving two bleeding wounds. But Kablaya continued to dance for a while. Since he was so old, his helpers watched closely. When they felt it was time, they rushed up to him and helped him out of the lodge.

With the next dancer and the next the helpers followed the same procedure of piercing the dancer's body. These helpers carried out the promise each dancer had made. They put twelve pegs into the body of the man who had offered twelve pieces of flesh to Wakan Tanka. Seeing her husband's suffering, the dancer's wife and his other relatives joined him in the dance. One woman offered her husband an herb, which she believed would lessen his pain. She placed the herb in his mouth, and the man chewed it. Long after the pegs had pulled out the promised pieces of flesh, he continued dancing, his head always up, staring at the sun.

As the dancers freed themselves and left the

dance lodge, they returned to the sweat lodge. Each received praise from Kablaya for his courage, and all were assured that everyone would remember their sacrifices on this day and that they would become leaders of their people.

7

WITHOUT THE BUFFALO

THROUGH the early part of the nineteenth century the relations between the Sioux and non-Indians were friendly. The Sioux were told in 1804, when Lewis and Clark passed through their lands, that the whites wanted to find an easy land route to the Pacific coast. Lewis and Clark assured the Sioux that the whites had no intention of settling on the barren plains. They wanted to settle the west coast and leave to the Indians the country between the East and the Far West. The Sioux were glad to get guns and ammunition from the white men, so they could hunt the buffalo more efficiently. They were glad to trade horses, buffalo robes, buckskin, and pemmican for these guns. The white man's articles—handsome saddles and horse trappings—pleased these lovers of horses. The beads, kettles, metal knives, and cloth were added luxuries at home. They were happy and content to meet the white traders and help them continue their journey westward.

On the plains to the south, the warlike Kiowa, Comanche, and Arapaho made sorties against the white men's mule trains and wagons—but more for the fun of raiding than because of need. They, too, felt no premonition of the white man's invasion of their lands.

By 1830, the prairie land to the east of the Dakotas was being divided up into states. The Missouri and Osage tribes were forced out of their lands. For twenty more years settlers continued to press westward. In 1849, the United States War Department, which had heretofore protected the settlers against Indians, turned the job over to the Department of the Interior. The immediate task of the Department was to settle the Indians on reservations and to make treaties with the various

Plains Indian groups. The mighty Dakota were soon embroiled in the confusion of treaty making.

The Sioux were intelligent and able people, so their confusion was all the more understandable. If the government failed to keep the terms of a treaty, the Sioux felt the treaty was broken and that they had the right to act as though none ex-·isted. They did not want to give up the lands in the first place. Pretty soon they were in great trouble with the settlers and the United States Government.

On April 29, 1868, the Sioux signed a treaty, agreeing to live on a reservation in the Territory of the Dakotas. The reservation was to include some 34,125 square miles, and was named the Great Sioux Reservation. All the Sioux, who numbered then about 25,000, were to settle on it. The government assured the Sioux that this land was to be theirs forever. No part of this reserve would ever be taken from the Sioux, unless three quarters of their adult population signed in favor of it. Furthermore, no individual to whom land had been given would ever be told to leave his land without his personal consent. But somehow, within fifteen years, much of the land assigned to the Sioux under this treaty slipped from their hands into the possession of white settlers.

The Sioux loved the Black Hills. They went to them from the plains during the hot summers to cool off. Their women gathered and dried the abundant harvests of berries, which lasted them for the rest of the year. The men hunted and cut tipi poles. It was agreed between the Sioux and the United States Government that no one should enter the Black Hills without the permission and consent of the Dakota.

Although he was aware of this treaty, the dashing, long-haired General George Armstrong Custer, with some 1200 men, did enter the Black Hills in 1874. Custer and his men were overwhelmed with the beauty of these hills—the meadows covered with carpets of flowers, the crystal-clear streams, the fertile soil, the parks and valleys. "Their equal I have never seen," General Custer wrote in his report to Congress.

Custer also reported that he had met a small

camp of Sioux Indians and had offered them gifts of coffee, flour, and sugar. It was a very small Sioux camp of only five tipis, and the Indians knew they were no match against over a thousand men. They were afraid to talk to Custer and tell him that he was trespassing on their sacred lands, so they refused his gifts and fled. Custer sent scouts after them, but the Indians refused to turn back. A skirmish followed. An Indian was wounded, but continued running. Custer continued exploring the forbidden territory, feasting, as he reported in detail, on wild raspberries, strawberries, currants, blueberries, and wild cherries, and shooting game. Custer and his men also inspected the clear streams, and in another report to Congress, he came up with the news that "gold has been found in several places. I have on my table forty or fifty particles of pure gold."

This news somehow leaked out. The trek to the Black Hills for gold began. In vain General Philip H. Sheridan, who was in charge of the army, wired General Alfred H. Terry, in charge of the Dakota Territory, to keep miners out of the Black Hills. The tide of gold miners was not stemmed. It continued through 1874 and 1875. For a time the army stopped them by guarding all entrances to the Black Hills, and only a few sneaked in. In the meantime, government commissioners tried to make a treaty with the Indians for the lease of the Black Hills. But it did not work out. The Indians wanted more money than the government was willing to pay.

While the negotiations were going on, in 1875, the army's watch of the roads relaxed, and miners poured in. In the spring of 1876, the Sioux chiefs decided to go on the warpath. Warriors began to slip from their camps, leaving their wives, children, and old men behind.

On June 17, 1876, Chief Crazy Horse and his Oglala men fought General Crook, and won the battle. But instead of following up the victory, the Sioux slipped away to join a larger force. It is estimated that some 2500 Sioux gathered quietly in the valleys of the Little Big Horn in Montana.

Custer must have been entirely unaware of the gathering of these Sioux warriors. As he descended into the valley with his men, they were surrounded and wiped out. It all happened very fast. Some historians say the battle may have taken only ten minutes. The Sioux counted their dead at about sixty men, but they celebrated that night with a scalp dance.

Many versions of this battle have been written, but actually not many details are known, except for the gruesome results—a column of men destroyed within minutes!

In the morning the Sioux attacked another army column, which was on its way to help Custer, but stopped fighting at nightfall, broke camp, and moved toward the Big Horn mountains.

Sioux skirmishes with whites continued after the Custer battle, but none on as large a scale. Soon the reservation Sioux began to trickle back to their agencies. En route to the agency, wherever they came upon a train of white settlers or a white settlement, they attacked and raided it for goods and horses. Sitting Bull and several other chiefs, with about 100 to 150 warriors, moved in the meantime toward the Canadian border to escape. They knew the army would seek revenge. General Nelson A. Miles, who chased after them, managed to get the surrender of five chiefs, but Sitting Bull crossed into Canada.

The following winter Crazy Horse and his band, some 900 people with 2000 ponies, finally returned to the agency. But when spring came, Crazy Horse and his men began to chafe in the confinement of the reservation. Suspicious of his plans, the army surrounded him. When they tried to imprison him, Crazy Horse drew his knife and started to fight his way through the guards. He was mortally wounded, and died on September 5, 1877. These Sioux were then moved, along with Chief Spotted Tail and Chief Red Cloud, to the Missouri River, but Crazy Horse's men struck out for the Powder River country.

Later, Spotted Tail and his people and Red Cloud and his people became dissatisfied with their location on the Missouri. Red Cloud established himself at the Pine Ridge Agency, Spotted

RED CLOUD

SITTING BULL

SPOTTED TAIL

CRAZY HORSE

Tail at the Rosebud Agency. In 1881, Sitting Bull returned to the United States, and settled at the Standing Rock Agency.

By this time the buffalo herds had disappeared. The last buffalo hunt took place in 1882. The Sioux were bewildered, as though the earth had been pulled out from under them. A giant hand had closed the legendary cave from which the buffalo used to emerge each spring.

The Sioux did not blame themselves for this disappearance. They blamed the non-Indians for their excessive, wasteful hunting. Buffalo robes and skins were in great demand by the whites. But the Sioux had at all times followed the prescribed ritual of the Sun Dance. They welcomed the herds each spring and thanked Tatanka—the buffalo spirit—after every hunt for its gift to the people that they might live. The only solution the Sioux saw was to unite and rid their plains of the white settlers, so the buffalo might emerge again, as in the good, rich past. Without the buffalo, the Sioux and the other plains people faced starvation. They knew of no other way to make a living.

With the buffalo gone, and deer and elk scarce too, the Sioux fell back more and more upon the rations the government provided. The treaty of 1868 had promised to provide food, clothing, farm tools, and cattle, so the Sioux could support themselves on a reservation. Beef, coffee, flour, and sugar were allotted to each family. These allotments were to continue till the Sioux turned into farmers and were able to raise their own food. The land around each reservation was accordingly broken up into chunks of 160 acres and given to each Sioux family to farm. Unfortunately, the Sioux men, skilled in hunting, were ignorant about farming. Besides, in their traditions, the women were the ones to do the heavy work. It was unbecoming for a man to do women's work. So most men did nothing.

While the rations lasted, families shared and ate their fill, as they had done in the days when buffalo were abundant. If anyone in the village happened to be on hand when a family received its ration, he was welcome to share it. When the rations were gone and it was not yet time to get new rations, the Sioux tightened their belts and did with less and less. Children sickened, and the women were kept busy caring for them and doing the sewing, mending, and cooking. But the fathers sat at home doing nothing. Gradually these proud and intelligent hunters grew into dull, lazy, aimless men.

People were dying. The population was decreasing. So in 1882 the Secretary of the Interior began to negotiate with the Sioux for a change in the existing treaties and for an agreement to release some 17,000 acres of land—almost half the Dakota reserve—that they were not using. This land was to be sold to white settlers. It was reported that the government expected to get at least $5,000,000 from homesteaders for this land. In exchange, the Department of the Interior planned to present the Indians with 25,000 cows and 1000 bulls, so they could start raising cattle. At the cost of some $35 per cow and about $50 per bull, this would cost the Department only about $925,000.

The Dakota were unaware of the sums and the profits involved. They refused to sign away the lands for a different reason. It was a custom among the Sioux to bring gifts when making treaties among themselves. Accordingly, they demanded that the 25,000 cows and 1000 bulls be delivered at once. When the cattle failed to arrive, the Sioux complained to their agents that the government had failed to keep its promise and that they would, therefore, sign no treaties.

Matters were at a standstill in 1883, when the

government commissioners arrived to talk with the Sioux. The commissioners were ignorant of some Indian customs. They asked the agents to send messengers to call the Indians together. When the Sioux arrived, the commissioners proceeded to ask them questions, expecting replies. The Indians refused to talk. Their custom for discussions in council followed a different procedure. First, they wanted to hear the questions. Then they sat in small groups to discuss the questions among themselves, to decide what to answer, and to select a spokesman—usually a chief and good orator—to give the answers before the assembled audience.

A long, embarrassing silence followed each commissioner's question. Finally Sitting Bull, as the most respected of the assembled chiefs, got up to explain the trouble to the commissioners. But the commissioners were confused by the silence of the assembled Indians, and they were impatient with Sitting Bull, because they considered him responsible for the Custer massacre.

As Sitting Bull arose to speak, he naturally

asked the commissioners whether they knew who he was. The commissioners could not hide their bitterness. They replied that they did know who he was. He was an Indian, like the rest of the Indians present.

This reply stung Sitting Bull to the quick. He spoke with the pride and boastfulness of a successful Sioux warrior and chief. Addressing his own people as well as the whites, Sitting Bull said, "These white men do not know who I am. Well, I will tell them. I am here by the will of the Great Spirit, and by his will, I am a chief. Yet you men have come here to talk with us and you say you do not know who I am.

"I want to tell you that if the Great Spirit had chosen anyone to be the chief of this country, it would be myself. But since you do not know me, it is best for us to leave this council."

Sitting Bull turned to leave. All the Indians followed him, proving to the commissioners that Sitting Bull still held power. Their departure also gave the Sioux a chance to decide among themselves on a course of action.

When the Sioux and the commissioners met again, Sitting Bull said, "Since the Great Father wants the Sioux to live like white men, his people would like to have the things the white men have. They would like more food. They would like homes that are warm in winter. They would like cattle, sheep, hogs. I want some agricultural implements, so that I will not be obliged to work bare-handed. Our rations have been reduced to almost nothing, and the people have starved to death in winter. Look at the men around here, and see how poorly dressed they are. We want some clothing this month. When it gets cold we want more of it to protect us from the weather. That is all I have to say."

Sitting Bull's speech helped bring into the open the resentment of the Sioux. Other speakers followed, and the commissioners listened for many days to their testimony. It became clear that the Sioux had been threatened with the loss of their rations, their religion, and their homes near the agencies. It was also brought out that in order to get a long list of signatures on a treaty, the agents had school children sign.

When the commissioners finally returned to Washington to report these findings, little could be done about it. The treaties had been in effect for some time. The Sioux had also fought against the United States, and so the loss of their lands was considered a fair forfeit. The government hoped for more fair treatment of these people in the future, but it could not mend the past.

The Sioux, too, were looking for a way out. The solution to their plight lay in a new hope—in the outcome of the Ghost Dance religion. This new belief promised the Plains Indians, if they followed the ritual for the dance, that the Great Spirit would destroy all white men. The lands and freedom to move about would then be restored to all Indians. Furthermore, if they followed the ritual, their dead ancestors would return to life, and the buffalo herds would again roam the plains. The people would forever enjoy happiness, good health, eternal youth, and plenty.

The vision that started the Ghost Dance came to Wovoka, a Paiute Indian near Pyramid Lake in Nevada. This Indian dreamed on January 1, 1889, during an eclipse of the sun, that he went up to heaven and saw the Great Spirit and all his dead relatives. They all looked young and happy. Some were hunting; others played games; others danced. Heaven was full of buffalo, deer, and elk. The Great Spirit told Wovoka to return to earth and tell his people to dance for four nights. On the fifth day, after an all-night dance, the people must bathe and go home.

The Great Spirit further said, "Dance every six weeks, feast, and enjoy good food. Be good. Be truthful. Live in peace among yourselves as well as with the whites. But do not tell the whites of this vision. The whites will disappear, and the land will be left to the Indians."

Within six months, news of this vision reached the Sioux. They called a council of chiefs. Among them were Red Cloud, American Horse, Man-Afraid, and Sitting Bull. The council selected men to go to Wovoka to learn more about this vision. The men sent word to their people that there was great excitement among the western Indians. People were now saying that within a year the whites would be wiped out. The buffalo, as well as their dead ancestors, would return. Despite warnings from the white agents in charge, the Sioux started to dance too.

The preparations for a Ghost Dance resembled somewhat the preparations for a Sun Dance. Men fasted and purified themselves in sweat lodges. They planted a small tree in the center of a dance lodge. The dance began before sundown, and the time was announced by messenger. The leaders entered the lodge first and, joining hands, began to circle around the tree. The songs were first whispered by the dancers, then shouted. Again, a woman held the calumet while the people danced, but this time she faced west instead of east toward the rising sun. If a man or a woman became excited, as though he or she was about to see a vision, friends led the person away, so he might rest and sleep. More and more people joined the Ghost

Dance. Within a year—by 1890—they were dancing the Ghost Dance on all Sioux reservations.

Things had been particularly bad for the Siouan people. There was drought on the plains, so even those among the Sioux who farmed a little had nothing to harvest. There was a feeling in the government that if the Sioux were hard-pressed for food, they would try harder to farm. So the government cut rations still further. The Sioux were confused, since the treaties promised that the government would keep supplying them with food as long as they needed it. And they needed food and clothing. Perhaps it would help the Great Spirit to exterminate the whites if the Sioux went on the warpath.

The whites must have been warned of this. Late in November of 1890, about 3000 troops were sent in to all the reservations. Some of the Sioux panicked and fled to the Badlands in South Dakota. Those who remained were forbidden to dance. Rations were now resumed. Sitting Bull, who favored the Ghost Dance, was watched. On

December 15, 1890, he was surrounded by the Siouan police, because they thought he wanted to leave camp. In the scuffle that took place, he was shot and killed by two Indian policemen.

In view of the hostility of the whites, it seemed more urgent than ever to continue the Ghost Dance. The faith of the Sioux in Wovoka's vision never wavered. They were sure that the whites would disappear, and so they continued dancing. They were also convinced that by wearing special buckskin shirts they were safe from bullets. Except for one incident of killing a white man, there were no attacks on whites during this period. Rather, the Sioux avoided provoking an encounter with any of the settlers.

They readily gave up their arms, as the troops demanded, but the soldiers continued searching. They entered a Sioux camp at Wounded Knee to look for more weapons. This frightened the camp. Women and children inside the tipis were horrified—especially when the soldiers began to handle the bedrolls and the Indians' personal possessions in search of guns and ammunition. The

Indian men were also tense and frightened. Suddenly someone fired a shot. A young Sioux pulled a gun from his blanket and fired too. Although the soldiers had no instructions from their superiors to use guns, they did so now. Their first shots killed half the Siouan warriors. A field gun had been set up, overlooking the camp. It now began to discharge volley after volley right into the camp, killing and wounding mostly women and children. The remaining Indians now joined the battle. Those who had no guns used their war clubs and knives very effectively in the close fighting.

This battle took place on December 29, 1890, and is known to history as the Battle of Wounded Knee. Over 300 Indians were killed that day and about 60 white soldiers. But it marked the last battle between the Sioux and the United States Army.

On the day following the Battle of Wounded Knee, the Sioux warriors slipped out of their camps. They burned the homes of the whites along their routes, but did not kill anyone.

CANADA

MONTANA

NORTH DAKOTA

MINNESOTA

Yellowstone R.

Missouri River

Powder River

•Bismark

Farqo•

Wahpetoo School o

San Arcs Sioux

STANDING ROCK

o Fort Yates

SISSETON

CHEYENNE RIVER

•Mobridge

•Laplant

Sisseton

SOUTH DAKOTA

BLACK HILLS

•Deadwood
•Lead
o Rapid City

Pierre•

CROW CREEK

Pipestoneo School

•Pipeston•

•Custer

PINE RIDGE

ROSEBUD

YANKTON

IOWA

WYOMING

Wounded Knee

•Martin

oRosebud

Sioux City

Pine Ridge

SANTEE

NEBRASKA

Platte River

COLORADO

SIOUX LANDS

Reservations   • { State Capitals
o Schools   { and Towns

*   *   *

The nature of the Great Plains is such that it is better cattle country than farming country. But cattle do not supply all the needs the Sioux have today, as the buffalo did a century ago. The Indians had to learn more efficient farming and stock raising, which would give them a cash income. Agricultural programs were introduced early by the government schools to train the young Sioux to become modern farmers. Where reservation land was good for grazing only, as at Pine Ridge, for example, boys were trained as ranchers and cowboys. They had to learn to rope cattle, brand and dehorn it in the spring, and to drill wells and build windmills. Teams of boys went out to care for the cattle on the range. A boy learned to spend an entire day in the saddle, make camp, and care for himself in the open.

Girls were taught domestic science. The Siouan women were always hard workers. They could do almost anything with their hands.

Book learning became important, because boys and girls had to learn more about white people—

their history, laws, and religion—so that they would know more about the lands they owned and be able to utilize their property to the fullest. They also wished to live and to get along with white people.

At present the problems that face these Sioux are the same problems that face any people whose means are limited. On the reservations they live in rural slum conditions. Most of the houses are little one-room log cabins. There is no plumbing, running water is unknown, and electricity is rare. Since their lands are for the most part poor and overgrazed, it is difficult to raise cattle profitably. Some families have let their lands go and have moved to cities. But it is not easy for them to earn a living there, because they lack the special skills they need. Many such families end up seeking government relief.

The schools on the reservations are improving now, and new ones are being built. Better roads are also being built, as well as new homes. The children are beginning to be taught by people who know more about their background and who are

aware of the skills they will need later in life. The parents are also being helped to make their lives more productive and their communities better places in which to live.

Siouan chiefs today are working hard with their tribal councils to find ways to improve the lot of their people. One Siouan chief, named William Whirlwind Horse, recently summed up his people's feelings and aims when he said, "We want to raise the standards of our people and change some attitudes. But we still want to be Indians."

INDEX

*Indicates illustrations

158 INDEX

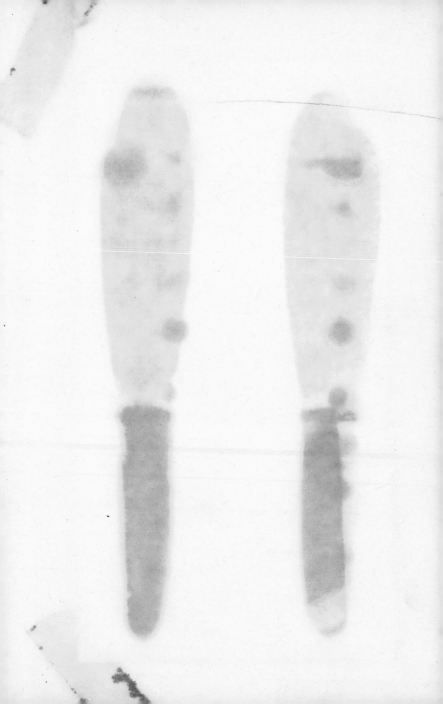

The Sioux Indians
Date Due

4/6			
8/5	11/10		
31ª30	12/2/95		
Jineb	12/14/95		
JUNE 1			
June 8			
3/23/92			
11/2/92			
11/7/92			
April 5			